COLOR & CRAFT
PYSANKI EASTER EGGS

Traditional Ukrainian Easter Egg Designs on Keepsake Paper Crafts to Color

EASY PRE-PRINTED PAPER CRAFTS TO COLOR, CUT, GLUE AND MAKE
The Anni Arts coloring crafts are ready to color and craft in this book format.
'Print-on-demand' makes printing as environmentally friendly as printing the crafts at home.

CONTENT
EQUIPMENT GUIDE
3D EGG INSTRUCTIONS
ABOUT PYSANKI EGGS
PROJECTS TO COLOR AND MAKE

GREETING CARDS

5" x 7"/12.5 x 17.5cm *card toppers to color for art cards or to frame as reusable Easter décor*
SIX PYSANKI EGG CARD TOPPERS in Black and White Line: – *Color in any choice of colors.*
FOUR PYSANKI EGG CARD TOPPERS in Gray Line: – *Great for Pastel Colors*
FOUR PYSANKI EGG CARD TOPPERS with Black areas: – *Add the traditional Pysanki colors of yellow and red.*
Download a free blank template for a 5" x 7" card to print as card bases for the card toppers

DÉCOR

3D EGG-SHAPED EASTER DECORATIONS: – *An Anni Arts Design for seven unique egg-shaped decorations*
TWO EGG-SHAPED ROUNDED DECORATIONS: – *An Anni Arts Design for rounded egg-shaped decorations*
FESTIVE BUNTING/FLAGS/PENNANTS: – *To color and use as keepsake décor on a wall or over a door or window. Store the bunting in a large envelope to protect them for many years of Easter displays.*
TAGS: – *Double-layered for the required thickness for tags. Cut to an egg shape and punch a hole for a tag.*
EGG WRAPS: – *Use to wrap eggs or make an egg stand with the broad border element.*

BONUS DOWNLOADS for PRINTABLE PROJECTS at **www.anniarts.com/pysanki-clip-art**
Paper for small gifts; Card Topper; Tag; Label; Blank Templates for card bases

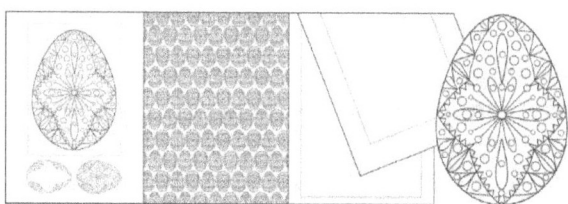

More printable craft freebies of all kinds can be downloaded from **Anni Arts Crafts www.anniartscrafts.com**

OTHER PYSANKI EGG PRODUCTS

- See the coordinating *Pysanki Egg Cut-N-Make Book* with pre-printed paper crafts in traditional Pysanki folk colors. The items are ready to cut, make and glue for Cards and Décor.
- Pysanki Egg designs are also on the printable Anni Arts 3D Paper Craft Mug and 3D Egg Decorations.
- Ready-to-buy products with the traditional Ukrainian Easter eggs and colors, like mugs and items for Easter celebrations, wishes and gifts are in the Anni Arts Zazzle store. Anni Arts Pysanki fabrics are on Spoonflower.
Follow links from the book's page on Anni Arts. www.anniarts.com

EQUIPMENT

Only a few basic items are needed to make these creative paper crafts for Easter.

PENCIL CRAYONS, MARKERS or COLORED BALL POINT PENS
SCISSORS
CRAFT KNIFE with a sharp blade to cut straight lines (optional)
RULER (With a metal edge if used with a craft knife)
GLUE STICK
ADHESIVE TAPE (Use as an alternative to glue on some items, like the egg wraps.)
If you use tape, double-sided tape will be preferable as it can be concealed.
PAPER SCORER
The bunting flags and tags have lines to be scored and folded.

A paper scorer is an instrument to draw a line to make folding that line easier.
It makes a dent on the card or paper, but does not cut right through. It is essential for creating tidy and precise paper crafts. Craft shops sell special scoring instruments, but an empty ballpoint pen is just as efficient - and is my personal favourite! You can also use the blunt side of the blade of a craft knife to make a *very light* score. And in a pinch you can also use a butter knife (with no serrations on the blade).
Note: When scoring regular paper like that used in this paper craft book, take care to score lightly – the paper can easily tear if the score runs too deep.

TIPS AND GENERAL INSTRUCTIONS

All pages have the relevant instructions printed with the paper craft item.

TIPS
First cut each craft page from the book along the guide line. A craft knife is handy for this.
Color before cutting and making the Cards, Bunting, 3D Decorations and Egg Wraps.
Score all lines as indicated on the bunting.
Cut out the shape of the pre-printed card element or craft template.
Fold on the scored lines and glue or assemble as indicated.

GREETING CARDS
Make sure that glue goes all the way to the edges of the card elements. Lay a blank piece of paper over a freshly positioned and glued element and glide the edge of a ruler over the covered section to flatten and properly glue the element to the underlying layer. The cover paper protects the coloring and the glued elements.

The topper patches are glued to blank cards cut from cardstock.
Cut card bases to the dimensions given below, *or download the printable blank templates from Anni Arts* and print the card bases on printable cardstock at the link below. The card toppers can also be glued to postcards on a single card layer. The cards need purchased envelopes. Labels and border designs can be used to decorate envelopes.

*Cut a **10" x 7" (approx. 25.5 x 17.75 cm)** backing for a card that folds to **5" x 7"** (or cut a 5" x 7" postcard)*
Score through the middle to fold the card and add the card making elements to the front

Text, Book Layout, Cover, Illustrations and Crafts by Anneke Lipsanen.
Copyright Anneke Lipsanen. All Rights Reserved. No part of this publication may be reproduced, or transmitted in any form without prior written permission from Anneke Lipsanen. Paperback Edition 2022

UKRAINIAN FOLK EASTER EGGS

People have been decorating eggs for thousands of years.
Long before the Christian era, eggs were revered as symbols of fertility. They were believed to embody great powers and were decorated to celebrate the return of the sun, warmth and growth in Spring. The sun was the focus of the early historical designs and the other patterns developed over centuries. Later, the ancient traditions were absorbed into the new Christian customs, resulting in a mixture of old and newer designs - like the fish and the cross.

There are two types of Ukrainian eggs. The *Krashanka* are boiled, edible eggs in one bright color that is most often red. The *Pysanki* eggs are raw, multi-colored and ornamental eggs. Great care goes into the lavish decorations and many of the motifs still used today have been in continuous use throughout the history of Pysanki eggs.

The Pysanki eggs eventually dry out - and with care can be kept indefinitely. Duck, goose or hens' eggs can be used. Traditionally, a bowl of decorated eggs was kept in the home for health, happiness, fertility and good fortune.

Pysanki eggs are decorated using the wax resist method using bee's wax and dye. The *Kistka* is the instrument used to draw on the egg with the melted bee's wax. Lines drawn in wax do not take up color. A spoon is used to lower an egg into a wide-mouthed jar with a solution of dye. A candle flame is used to melt the wax on the egg and a cloth used to wipe the egg, revealing the beautiful patterns and colors.

The traditional colors for Pysanki eggs are white, yellow, red and black, with orange and green used to a lesser degree. Orange can be obtained from over dying yellow with red. White is essentially the color of the egg itself.

Earlier, the dyes were prepared from organic materials. Yellow was obtained from onion skins or buckwheat husks; red from cochineal or deer horn; black from the husks of sunflower seeds with the addition of sulphate of iron. Green could be made from wild elder berries. Modern Pysanki eggs are dyed with synthetic dyes in a wide range of vivid traditional and non-traditional colors.

Designs fall into three categories: plants, animals and geometric designs. In recent years it has become customary to personalize the eggs with names and messages.

The words 'Khristos Voskres' (*Christ is Risen*) is chanted by the priest, choir and congregation during the Resurrection church service at Easter. And Pysanki eggs are exchanged with those words when people greet another after the service.

It is believed that as long as the tradition of the Pysanki eggs remains
and eggs continue to be decorated, the world will continue to exist.

Get bonus Pysanki egg crafts to color, plus other printable items for free at www.anniarts.com/pysanki-clip-art

Get bonus Pysanki egg crafts to color, plus other printable items for free at www.anniarts.com/pysanki-clip-art

Get bonus Pysanki egg crafts to color, plus other printable items for free at www.anniarts.com/pysanki-clip-art

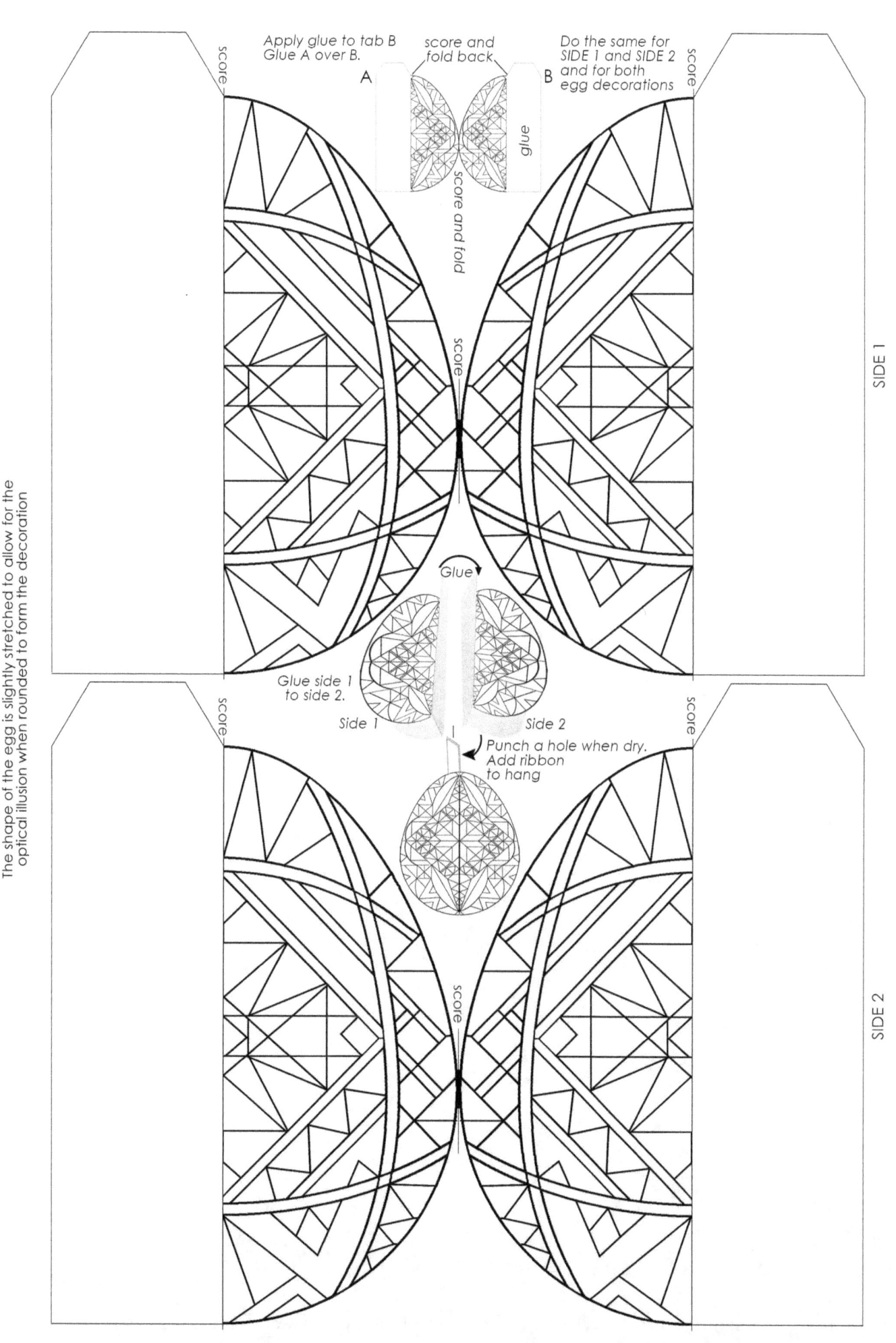

Get bonus Pysanki egg crafts to color, plus other printable items for free at www.anniarts.com/pysanki-clip-art

Get bonus Pysanki egg crafts to color, plus other printable items for free at www.anniarts.com/pysanki-clip-art

CARD TOPPERS: BLACK and WHITE LINES. Color egg and background (optional). Cut egg shape or entire rectangular background and glue to cardstock.

CARD TOPPERS: BLACK and WHITE LINES. Color eggs and background (optional). Cut egg shape or entire rectangular background and glue to cardstock.

Get bonus Pysanki egg crafts to color, plus other printable items for free at www.anniarts.com/pysanki-clip-art

CARD TOPPERS: BLACK and WHITE LINES. Color egg and background (optional). Cut egg shape or entire rectangular background and glue to cardstock.

Get bonus Pysanki egg crafts to color, plus other printable items for free at www.anniarts.com/pysanki-clip-art

CARD TOPPERS: GRAY LINES - BEST for PASTELS. Color egg and background (optional). Cut egg shape or entire rectangular background and glue to cardstock.

Get bonus Pysanki egg crafts to color, plus other printable items for free at www.anniarts.com/pysanki-clip-art

CARD TOPPERS: GRAY LINES - BEST for PASTELS. Color egg and background (optional). Cut egg shape or entire rectangular background and glue to cardstock.

Get bonus Pysanki egg crafts to color, plus other printable items for free at www.anniarts.com/pysanki-clip-art

CARD TOPPERS: BLACK DETAIL. Pre-filled black. Color egg and background (optional). Cut egg shape or entire rectangular background and glue to cardstock.

Get bonus Pysanki egg crafts to color, plus other printable items for free at www.anniarts.com/pysanki-clip-art

CARD TOPPERS: BLACK DETAIL. Pre-filled black. Color egg and background (optional). Cut egg shape or entire rectangular background and glue to cardstock.

Get bonus Pysanki egg crafts to color, plus other printable items for free at www.anniarts.com/pysanki-clip-art

Get bonus Pysanki egg crafts to color, plus other printable items for free at www.anniarts.com/pysanki-clip-art

Get bonus Pysanki egg crafts to color, plus other printable items for free at www.anniarts.com/pysanki-clip-art

DECORATIVE BORDERS for EGG WRAPS or STANDS and TAGS

The completed tags are egg-shaped. Score each tag. Fold double. Glue whole surface area on inside of tag. Flatten. Cut to an egg shape once dry. Punch hole.

Get bonus Pysanki egg crafts to color, plus other printable items for free at www.anniarts.com/pysanki-clip-art